For my three colorful guys and the fuzzy golden girl.
J.P.

Broadman & Holman Publishers
127 Ninth Avenue, North, Nashville, TN 37234
© 1998 Ottenheimer Publishers, Inc.

Cover and interior design by Susan L. Chamberlain

Printed and bound in Italy.
SB133 M L K J I H G F E D C B A
ISBN: 0-8054-1718-4

All God's Colors

Poem by Patricia Tower
Pictures by Judith Pfeiffer

**Do you think
God made the dark
so we could see the light?**

Or was it so
we'd always know
the daytime from the night?

And did he give us colors just to make the world confusing?

**Or did he think we'd find
the colors lovely and amusing?**

Did he make the flowers
in all colors just for fun?

Or was it that he loved them all,
and couldn't choose just one?

Did he put the stripes and spots on tigers and giraffes

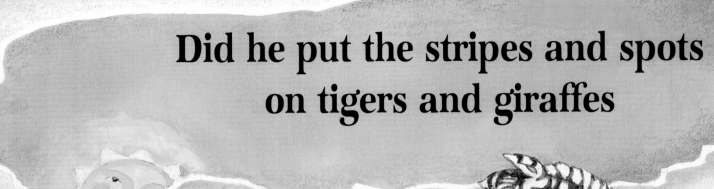

Because they looked so wonderful,
they made God smile and laugh?

And when God made the penguins, skunks and pandas black and white,

Do you think he said out loud,
"One color's not quite right"?

**Now, do you have a favorite color?
One that you can name?**

**Or do you love them as God does—
all colors just the same?**